D0478443

Weightlifting

GETTING THE EDGE: CONDITIONING, INJURIES, AND LEGAL & ILLICIT DRUGS

Baseball and Softball
Basketball
Cheerleading
Extreme Sports
Football
Gymnastics
Hockey
Lacrosse
Martial Arts
Soccer
Track & Field
Volleyball
Weightlifting
Wrestling

Weightlifting

by J. S. McIntosh

Mason Crest Publishers

MASON CREST PUBLISHERS INC.
370 Reed Road
Broomall, Pennsylvania 19008
(866)MCP-BOOK (toll free)
www.masoncrest.com

First Printing
9 8 7 6 5 4 3 2 1

Library of Congress Cataloging-in-Publication Data

McIntosh, J. S.
Weightlifting / by J. S. McIntosh.
p. cm.
Includes bibliographical references and index.
ISBN 978-1-4222-1742-9 ISBN (series) 978-1-4222-1728-3
1. Weight lifting. I. Title.
GV546.3.M3375 2011
613.7'13—dc22
2010017922

Produced by Harding House Publishing Service, Inc.
www.hardinghousepages.com
Interior Design by MK Bassett-Harvey.
Cover Design by Torque Advertising + Design.
Printed in the USA by Bang Printing.

Contents

Introduction

Getting the Edge: Conditioning, Injuries, and Legal & Illicit Drugs is a fourteen-volume series written for young people who are interested in learning about various sports and how to participate in them safely. Each volume examines the history of the sport and the rules of play; it also acts as a guide for prevention and treatment of injuries, and includes instruction on stretching, warming up, and strength training, all of which can help players avoid the most common musculoskeletal injuries. Each volume also includes tips on healthy nutrition for athletes, as well as information on the risks of using performance-enhancing drugs or other illegal substances. Getting the Edge offers ways for readers to healthily and legally improve their performance and gain more enjoyment from playing sports. Young athletes will find these volumes informative and helpful in their pursuit of excellence.

Sports medicine professionals assigned to a sport with which they are not familiar can also benefit from this series. For example, a football athletic trainer may need to provide medical care for a local gymnastics meet. Although the emergency medical principles and action plan would remain the same, the athletic trainer could provide better care for the gymnasts after reading a simple overview of the principles of gymnastics in Getting the Edge.

Although these books offer an overview, they are not intended to be comprehensive in the recognition and management of sports injuries. They should not replace the professional advice of a trainer, doctor, or nutritionist. The text helps the reader appreciate and gain awareness of the sport's history, standard training techniques, common injuries, dietary guidelines,

and the dangers of using drugs to gain an advantage. Reference material and directed readings are provided for those who want to delve further into these subjects.

Written in a direct and easily accessible style, GETTING THE EDGE is an enjoyable series that will help young people learn about sports and sports medicine.

—Susan Saliba, Ph.D., National Athletic Trainers' Association Education Council

1
The Basics of Weightlifting

Understanding the Words

aerobic: *Having to do with oxygen. Aerobic exercise requires more oxygen, so your heart and lungs have to work harder.*

physique: *The appearance and development of a person's physical body.*

comprehensive: *Including a large number of things; taking into account most important things.*

abdominals: *Referring to the muscles covering the abdomen, the lower half of the front of the human torso.*

lats: *Short for latissimus dorsi, the pair of large triangular muscles covering the middle and lower back.*

pectorals: *Referring to the muscle groups across the top of the chest.*

hydraulic resistance: *An opposing force created by the pressure of water or other fluid.*

reps: *Short for repetitions; repeated actions or sets of exercises.*

Weight training or weightlifting is popular for good reasons. Not only does it make you feel strong and improve your health, but it also makes you look slimmer and more toned and athletic. Looking good is important to many of us, but this should not be the main reason you take up weight training. Concentrating only on appearance may make you push your training forward faster than your body allows. That is when injuries happen. Instead, concentrate on weight training's clear health benefits:

- It builds up muscle strength, making muscles and joints less vulnerable to injury and disease.

Your muscles are actually made up of tiny fibers.

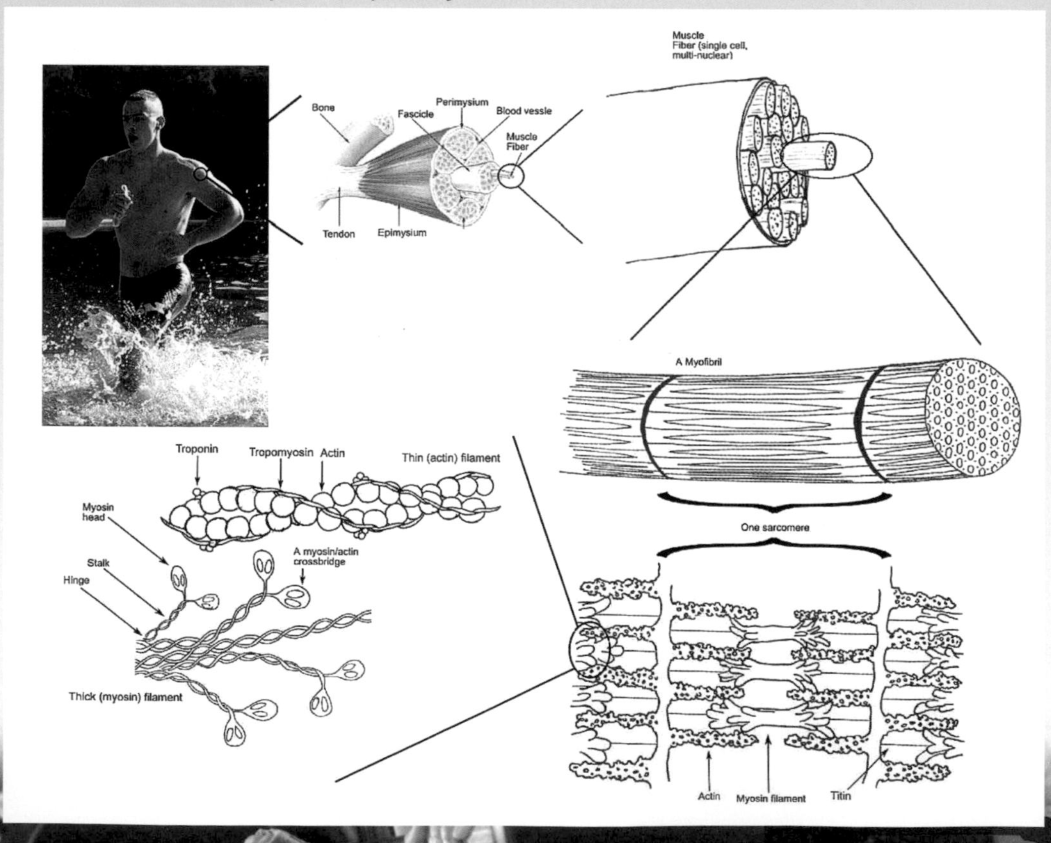

- When combined with a proper diet, it helps you to lose weight. Each pound of muscle in your body burns up thirty to forty calories a day. The more muscle you have, the more fat you lose.
- Weight training is a great way to control stress. It releases "feel good" chemicals in your body called endorphins, which give you a sense of well-being.
- It can make you physically stronger and more capable of safely handling heavy loads.
- It will help you perform better in other sports, boosting **aerobic** fitness and muscular power.

All these are excellent reasons to begin weight training.

Muscle Development

Your body has more than 600 muscles. Each muscle is built up of tiny fibers called myofibrils. When you need to perform a task requiring muscle power, your brain sends electrical orders to the muscle fibers via special nerve cells called neurons. The muscle fibers contract or expand according to the orders they receive from the brain.

Weight training results in improved strength and muscle bulk for several different reasons. First, the myofibrils respond to the weight training by growing thicker and stronger. Second, the actual number of myofibrils increases, expanding the size and power of the muscle. Finally, weight training improves the communication between the brain and the muscles.

We acquire any skill through practice, and doing weight training makes us more familiar with our bodies, giving us the balance, strength, and focus needed to lift heavy objects. For this reason alone, beginners at weight

Free weights are one way to build muscles. They are cheaper, versatile, and good for targeting specific muscles—but using free weights also makes you at greater risk of injury than if you were using a weight machine. (Photo by LocalFitness.com.au)

training develop additional strengths even before their muscles have started to grow.

Weight training does not necessarily require weights. Much good work can be done through age-old techniques such as push-ups, crunches, and triceps dips. These have the big advantage that you can do them anywhere:

in your living room, bedroom, or yard. Repeated every day in increasing numbers, such exercises will result in a strong **physique**. The muscle development using weightless exercises, however, is generally neither as fast nor as **comprehensive** as training using weights.

Options for Training

There are two systems of weights in strength training—free weights or weight machines. Free weights are simply heavy disks of metal (or, sometimes, weighted plastic), attached to a bar for lifting. There are generally two types of free weights: a dumbbell, which is designed to be held in one hand; or a long barbell, which is held in both hands. Combined with an exercise bench—a long, narrow bench, where you can lie or sit while lifting—free weights are sufficient for successful weight training.

Free weights have their pros and cons. The pros are:

- A huge number of different exercises can be performed with the most basic set of free weights.
- Free weights are excellent for working individual muscles.
- Free weights are far less expensive to buy than weight machines.

The disadvantages of free weights should not be overlooked, however:

- They are more difficult to use properly than weight machines because they require good balance. For this reason, you are more likely to injure yourself using free weights if you have not been trained in the correct technique;
- Doing free weights on your own can be dangerous—you run the risk of dropping them on yourself.

The alternative to free weights is weight machines. Weight machines are pieces of equipment scientifically designed to work specific groups of muscles. Therefore, there are weight machines for **abdominals**, **lats**, **pectorals**, and thigh muscles, along with others. A weight machine usually features a stack of weights, though some use systems of **hydraulic resistance** instead. For weight-stack machines, you select the weight you want to lift, pull, or push by putting a pin into a notch on the side of the stack. Weight machines can be extremely advanced, including ones that alter the resistance according to how tired your muscles become as you go through a set of **reps**. Other advantages include:

- They usually feature more weight options than free weights, so you can pick the level at which you want to train.
- They are safer to use because they are designed to hold you securely while training. You can usually lift more because you do not have to worry about balance.
- You do not need a spotter; if you are having problems lifting a weight, the machine will let you lower it safely to rest.

If you are trying to decide between weight machines and free weights, then don't—use both. Combining the two ensures a well-rounded physique and an endless variety of exercises.

Safe Training

Weight training can be done at home or in a local gym. Home training is very convenient; you can train whenever you want to, without having to travel. However, for someone new to weight training, the disadvantages of training at home outweigh the advantages.

JOINING A GYM

Look inside a gym before you join. The quality of its staff, equipment, and surroundings has an impact on your safety when you are training, so check the following points:

- Is the gym clean and well kept? Remember to also look in the showers and changing areas.
- Are all the pieces of gym equipment in good condition? Are free weights stacked in order of weight? Look out for things such as torn seating or frayed cables on the weight machines.
- Is the gym using weight machines made by reputable brands, such as Bodymaster or Nautilus? If you are not familiar with the names, ask a sports professional (such as an assistant in a professional sports shop) about them.
- Are the free weights free of rust?
- Is the atmosphere inside the gym friendly but disciplined?

Home training is often done unsupervised, so there is a greater danger of injuring yourself by using poor technique or the wrong type of equipment, or by lifting weights that are too heavy for you. Also, you have the expense of setting up a home gym. Simple free weights can be bought relatively inexpensively, but add on the weight bench and you might spend several hundred dollars. A complete weight machine center will easily cost you $800 to $1,000.

Another disadvantage is that people who train at home are more likely to give up. Exercising at home can be lonely and does not provide the motivation that comes from training around large groups of people.

Using a school or private gym solves these problems. A modern, well-equipped gym will contain a mix of both free weights and weight machines in large numbers. There will also be experts within the gym to advise on safe and effective technique. Most gyms will make you go through a short introductory course to teach you the basics of how to use the equipment. Some schools and colleges have gyms that are free of charge to the students.

Whether you choose to exercise at home or in a local gym, weight training is an excellent discipline to get you fit and in shape. "Discipline," however, is an important word. Your mind must be as fit and controlled as your body in order to get the most out of weight training.

Weight Lifting as a Sport

Weight training, as we know it, originated in the late nineteenth century. Gyms spread throughout Europe and the United States. Today, the International Weightlifting Federation (IWF) controls the competitive sport. Based in Budapest, it was founded in 1905.

OLYMPIC WEIGHT LIFTING

Weightlifting has an ancient history and became an Olympic sport in 1920. Women have also entered weightlifting. In 1987, the first all-female World Championship was held, and women's weightlifting became an Olympic sport in 2000.

Olympic-style weightlifting uses a barbell loaded with weight plates.

In Olympic weightlifting, participants attempt a maximum weight single lift of a barbell loaded with weight plates. The two lifts competed are the "clean and jerk" and the "snatch."

- The snatch involves lifting a weight straight from the floor to above the head in one movement. As the bar is lifted, the weight lifter drops down into a squatting position under the bar, while locking his arms to support the weights above him. Finally, he pushes himself up from the squatting position to a final standing position and holds the weight for a required length of time before lowering it.
- The clean and jerk differs because the weight lifter must first transfer the bar to shoulder height as he moves to the squatting position. This is the "clean" part of the technique. The "jerk" comes when the weight lifter pushes up with his legs and thrusts the weight above his head.

In both cases, the judges are looking for good technique as well as the heaviest weight lifted. Any errors in technique will result in points being deducted.

Competitors compete in one of eight divisions (seven for women), determined by their body mass. These classes for men are: 56 kg (123 lb), 62 kg (137 lb), 69 kg (152 lb), 77 kg (170 lb), 85 kg (187 lb), 94 kg (207 lb), 105 kg (231 lb), and over 105 kg. For women, the classes are: 48 kg (106 lb), 53 kg (117 lb), 58 kg (128 lb), 63 kg (139 lb), 69 kg (152 lb), 75 kg (165 lb), and over 75 kg. In each weight division, competitors compete in both the snatch and the clean and jerk. Prizes are usually given for the heaviest weights lifted in the snatch, clean and jerk, and the two combined.

The order of the competition is up to the lifters: the competitor who chooses to attempt the lowest weight goes first. If he is unsuccessful at that weight, he has the option of reattempting that lift or trying a heavier weight later (after any other competitors have made attempts at that weight or any intermediate weights). Weights are set in 1-kilogram increments, and each lifter can have a maximum of three lifts, regardless of whether lifts are successful or not.

The title "best lifter" is commonly awarded at local competitions. The award is based on the lifters' Sinclair Coefficients, which calculate strength-to-weight ratio of the lifters. Typically, the winner of the heaviest weight class will have lifted the most weight, but a lifter in a lighter weight class will have lifted more in proportion to his bodyweight.

Weightlifting is not a sport recommended for young people under eighteen years old. The strain it places on the muscles and skeleton is huge. The world's greatest weightlifters can haul over 440 pounds above their heads, but even weights a quarter of that should not be attempted by the young or the untrained. Weightlifters must also be extremely fit, as well as very strong. During each lift, the heart rate is pushed as high as 200 beats per minute, a dangerous level for those without advanced aerobic fitness.

BODYBUILDING

Bodybuilding is another competitive sport that developed out of weightlifting. In 1939, the first Mr. American competition was held under the auspices of the Amateur Athletic Union. Competitive bodybuilding went international in 1946 when Ben and Joe Weider—whose surname is often seen on weights and weight equipment—formed the International Federation of Body Building (IFBB). The IFBB promoted the art of bodybuilding in world competitions, including the prestigious Mr. Olympia and Ms. Olympia. Bodybuilding is not yet an Olympic event, although the International Olympic Committee is becoming more accepting of the sport.

Bodybuilding became popular as a sport in the United States in the 1930s, and has since grown into a massive international competitive activity, as well as a multi-million dollar industry. Both men and women practice the sport, many dreaming of becoming Mr. or Ms. Olympia, the supreme title in all bodybuilding.

Both men and women participate in bodybuilding.

A bodybuilding competition lets athletes demonstrate their muscle development in front of a panel of judges. In international competitions, under the International Federation of Body Building (IFBB), there are nine judges. Each competitor must perform “mandatory poses”—in other words, poses that they must display. There are seven mandatory poses for men and five for women. The poses are designed to display the six main muscle groups of the human body: arms, chest, abdomen, shoulders, backs, and legs. The bodybuilding is judged and scored according to four qualities: muscle definition, muscle density, muscle mass, and balanced muscular development.

ARNOLD SCHWARZENEGGER

Arnold Schwarzenegger is not only the governor of California and a Hollywood star, but also a legendary bodybuilder. Born in Graz, Austria, in 1947, he was fourteen when he began weight training, and only seventeen when he won his first trophy. In 1966, he won the Best Built Man in Europe, Mr. Europe, and the International Powerlifting Championship, although he failed to win his first Mr. Universe title. After designing new techniques to hone his body to perfection, he won the amateur Mr. Universe title in London in 1967 and added the professional title the next year.

Next, he moved to the United States, aiming to become Mr. Olympia. In 1970, he did. After that, he pursued a film career—and then moved on into politics. Arnold remains involved with fitness education. One of his key messages to young athletes is to avoid drugs and to enjoy a clean, healthy lifestyle.

Bodybuilding competitions are as much about art as strength. Men are obliged to shave their bodies of any hair concealing their muscles. Tanning products and oils are also used to highlight the contours of the body. Taking part in bodybuilding competitions requires a great deal of dedication. Several hours of training, for at least three days a week, are essential.

Body building isn't just about strength; many consider it an art form.

The opportunities to take part in bodybuilding competitions are huge. A large number of local, national, and international bodybuilding organizations exist and promote their own competitions. Your club, gym, or coach should be able to point you in the direction of beginners' competitions. If not, any good bodybuilding magazine provides a competition calendar.

POWERLIFTING

Bodybuilding is about the appearance of the athletes. Weightlifting is about sheer strength. And powerlifting is a fusion of bodybuilding and weightlifting.

The sport originated in bodybuilding gyms in the 1960s, when bodybuilders began to compete to see who could lift the heaviest weight. Today, powerlifting is an international sport, overseen by the International Powerlifting Federation (IPF).

There are three lifts in powerlifting: the bench press, squat, and dead lift. Like weightlifting, powerlifting is suitable only for adult competitors whose bodies have stopped growing. However, if you are interested in either sport, visit powerlifting or weightlifting websites or read magazines for more information about upcoming competitions. Watching competitions can teach you a lot about technique and etiquette, even if you are not training in the sport.

If, when you reach the right age for training, you are still interested in weightlifting or powerlifting, find a good team affiliated with a proper professional body such as U.S.A. Wrestling and International Powerlifting Federation.

2 Mental Preparation

Understanding the Words

cardiovascular: *Relating to the heart and blood vessels; cardiovascular exercise strengthens the heart muscle by increasing heart rate.*

pecs: *Short for pectorals, the muscles across the top of the chest.*

delts: *Short for deltoid muscles, the large triangular muscles covering the shoulder joint.*

traps: *Short for trapezius muscles, the large flat muscles running from the back of the neck to just below the shoulder blades.*

ligaments: *Bands of tissue connecting bones to each other.*

tendons: *Tough cords of tissue connecting muscles to bones.*

stroke: *A blockage or bleeding in a blood vessel leading to the brain, causing a part of the brain to die or be seriously damaged because of a lack of oxygen; depending on the location of the brain to be injured a stroke can lead to paralysis, weakness, speech difficulties, or death.*

aneurysm: *A weak spot in a blood vessel that can bulge outward and sometimes burst.*

synchronize: *To make things move, work, etc. at the same time and in the same way as each other.*

Weight training is an activity requiring mental discipline as much as physical discipline. One of the biggest challenges is to develop your strength gradually and safely, even when you are eager to push ahead quickly.

Injuries occur in weight training mainly because of careless technique or overly ambitious weight loading. Impatience is often the reason for this. Weight training has a rhythm to it. During the first six weeks of training—if you train regularly and properly—improvements to your physique can be quite rapid. Muscles in the arms, chest, and shoulders will tone and strengthen, and you may find you lose some weight. After this period, progress becomes slower. As your body strengthens, you will need to work harder to continue developing muscles.

When you struggle to put on more muscle, several things can happen. You may simply become discouraged and stop training. To counter this, focus on the improvements to your fitness rather than improvements to your appearance. However much you develop your muscles, there will always be someone bigger, more toned, and (in your eyes) more attractive.

If your only reason for doing weight training is to look good, ask yourself whether there is a deeper reason. Do you want people to respect you more? Do you want more attention from the opposite sex? You may have a poor self-image. Work out what it is you really want; simply putting on muscle bulk is unlikely to solve problems with self-image. Concentrate on the improvements in how you feel rather than on how you look. Enjoy the fact that you are getting fitter and stronger, and treat improvements in appearance as a bonus.

Of course, the other reason you might stop training is boredom. Weight training can be repetitive and monotonous, and if you are not seeing muscle

Why do you want big muscles? Being in top physical shape is a worthy goal, but your self-concept should not depend totally on your physical appearance.

gain, the inclination to stop training can be high. There are several things you can do to stop weight training from becoming boring:

- Vary your routines at the gym. If you concentrate on doing upper-body workouts one day, switch the next day to lower-body workouts, or spend more time on the cardiovascular machines.
- Shorten your workouts on some days. After a proper warm-up, you can do weights for just fifteen minutes and still get the benefit. In that time, you can do several exercises to work your legs, lats, **pecs**, **traps**, **delts**, and abdominals. Short routines are not for every time you go to the gym, but just for now and then, on those days when you really want to be somewhere else.
- Plan an enjoyable activity with your training partner for after the weights session. Following training with something exciting can make the training more exciting.

Steady Training

Weight training cannot be rushed. Do not make large jumps in the weights used. Adding ten pounds to your weight stack when you already struggle at the level where you are is a recipe for torn muscles, **ligaments**, and **tendons**. It can even result in a **stroke** caused by an **aneurysm**. Furthermore, do not over train by visiting the gym more often. During weight training, muscle fibers suffer microscopic tears from the effort. The fibers heal themselves in stronger configurations during periods of rest. If you do not have at least one day of rest between training days, this healing and muscle development cannot take place. Therefore, your muscles will be vulnerable to injury during training.

People under the age of eighteen should follow these training rules:

- Do not train more than three times a week.

Don't attempt to lift weights that are beyond your strength level. Always take time build up the weight you lift gradually, little by little.

EXERCISE FOR IMPROVING CONCENTRATION

Sit in front of a small object you have seen many times before—such as a pen or spoon—placed on a table. Make sure you are comfortable, and keep a watch or clock within view. Breathe slowly and stare at the object, examining it closely. Try to notice every detail: color, shape, texture, any damage, and so on. Your aim is to see things you have not noticed before. Do not let your concentration wander—keep looking. All of a sudden, you will see the object as if you are looking at it for the first time. That is the goal.

Practice for only five minutes at first. Next time, practice for ten minutes. Increase the time limit as far as your daily schedule will allow. If you can spend twenty to thirty minutes doing this, you will develop the right powers of concentration for your weight training.

- Keep training sessions under forty-five minutes—ideally closer to thirty minutes.
- When you first start on a particular machine or free weights exercise, practice the technique lifting no weight at all. Then lift weights under expert supervision until you can demonstrate perfect technique in up to fifteen repetitions.
- According to sports medicine experts Avery Faigenbaum and Wayne Westcott, the young weightlifter should add weights in increments of 1 to 3 pounds and perform one to three sets at the new weight. Once she can demonstrate perfect technique at the new weight, she may add further weights.

Another important ingredient for safe training is concentration. Whenever you lift, pull, or push a weight, focus all your attention on the muscle groups doing the work. If, for instance, you are doing a biceps curl exercise on a machine, concentrate on the slow curling action of your arms up toward our chest and then the release back down to the starting position. Feel what the muscles are doing throughout the lift, and move only your forearms; the rest of your body should be entirely still. To aid your concentration, **synchronize** your breathing with the action. Do not hold your breath, (which is a common mistake) because this deprives muscles of vital oxygen needed to work. Breathe out as you lift the weights to your chest, and inhale as you lower them. Maintaining concentration throughout a lift helps protect you from injuries caused by poor technique.

13
Preparing the Body

Understanding the Words

pliable: *Flexible, easily bent.*

repertoire: *A complete set of skills, abilities, etc. a person has in a certain field.*

groin: *The hollows on both sides of the front of the body where the thighs join the abdomen.*

gluteals: *The set of three muscles that make up the buttocks.*

Before each session of weight training, you have to prepare the body in order to reduce the risks of injury. Do this in two stages: warming up and stretching.

Some people arrive in a gym and rush straight to their favorite weight machine, lifting as much weight as they can. They are heading for the doctor. Weight training with cold and stiff muscles is a recipe for quick injury, mainly sprains and strains. Doing a proper warm-up routine will prepare your body for training. In turn, this means that each weight session will bring more progress.

Warming Up

A warm-up routine does exactly what it says—warms up the muscles, ligaments, and tendons of the body in preparation for exercise. A warm muscle is more **pliable** and flexible than a cold muscle, which means you can put it through an extended range of movement without damaging it.

Muscles also rely on oxygen to give them energy to work. Oxygen is carried to the muscles in the blood, and the blood picks up the oxygen as it passes through the lungs. During a warm-up routine, both breathing and heart rate are increased by light exercise. The overall effect is that we breathe in more air; more oxygen is delivered to the blood; and the blood pumps faster through the body.

A basic warm-up routine involves light exercise for between five and ten minutes, just enough to get slightly out of breath, raise the heartbeat, and warm up muscles. The key rule of a warm-up is not to do anything too strenuous but merely to prepare the muscles for exercise. Here is a typical warm-up routine:

1. Run very lightly on the spot without raising your knees too high. Shake your arms loosely by your sides to get rid of any stiffness in the arms and shoulders. Run for about two to three minutes, slightly increasing the pace and the height you raise the knees.

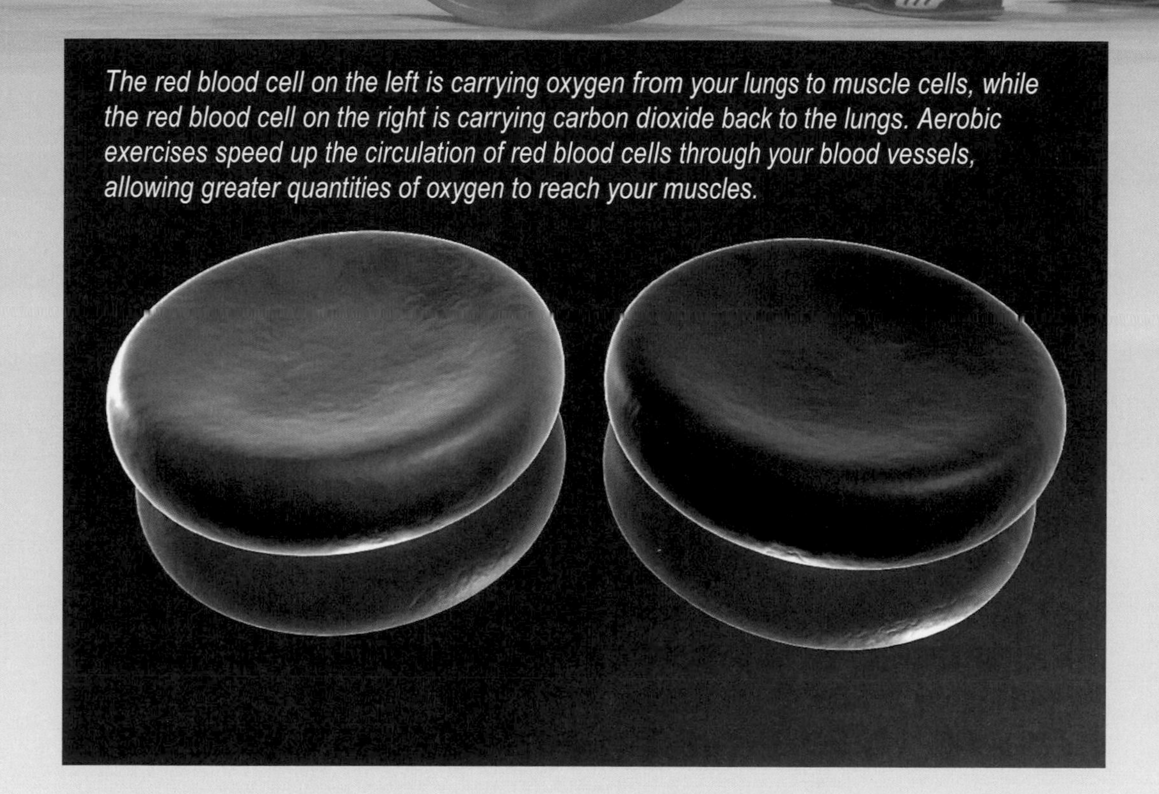

The red blood cell on the left is carrying oxygen from your lungs to muscle cells, while the red blood cell on the right is carrying carbon dioxide back to the lungs. Aerobic exercises speed up the circulation of red blood cells through your blood vessels, allowing greater quantities of oxygen to reach your muscles.

2. Stand up straight with your legs shoulder-width apart, looking straight ahead. Swing your arms forward in large circles about ten times, and then reverse the direction of the circles. Finally, swing the arms inward across your chest so that they cross each other, then outward again. Repeat ten times. This will warm up your shoulders.
3. To warm up your neck muscles, make large circles with your head in one direction about five times. Then reverse the direction for another five times. Brush your chest with your chin at the lowest point of the circle and stretch your head up rather than back at the top of the circle.

4. To warm up the leg and knee muscles, do about two minutes of lunges—stepping forward and then back with one leg, and repeating with the other. Do not push too hard, and make sure you bend your thigh so that it is at about a forty-five-degree angle to the floor.
5. Make large circles with your hips, first in one direction and then in the other. The circles should be as wide as possible, with your hands placed on your hips to facilitate the movement.
6. Finally, shake your entire body to loosen up and complete the warm-up. This warm-up does not use machines. In a gym you can warm up on some of the warm-up machines. The rowing machine, treadmill, stepper, and track machine (which imitates a skiing action) are all suitable. Try to combine two machines with different actions so that you warm up your entire body. A good combination would be the rowing machine and the stepper. Whatever machine you use, start at a gentle pace and work only hard enough to raise your breathing and temperature.

Once you have finished your warm-up, you can proceed to stretching.

Stretching

Flexibility is essential for almost every sport, including weight training. A weight-training session should work all the major muscle groups of the body so your flexibility preparation must do the same. There are a huge number of different stretches you can do. Ask a qualified sports coach, yoga teacher, or a similar flexibility expert to teach you a broad **repertoire** of techniques. Organize these into a specific routine that you will use before every weight-training session. Work from your feet to your head, or vice versa, so that you do not miss any muscles. It is important that you stretch any injured muscles or ligaments, until they are fully healed.

Here is a basic stretching routine:

1. Seated hamstring stretch: Sit on the floor with your legs stretched out in front of you and your back straight. Breathe in and bend forward from the waist until you can grip your ankles. Holding onto your ankles, bend farther forward until you feel a stretch along the calf muscles and the back of the knee. Hold the position for about ten seconds and then sit up slowly.

The same hamstring stretch that runners use to prepare for a race will help you achieve maximum flexibility for weightlifting.

2. Quadriceps stretch: Stand up straight, resting one hand against a wall for stability. Lift up your left leg behind you, then take hold of the top of the foot with your left hand and pull the heel up toward your buttocks. You should feel the stretch along the front of the thigh and the knee. Hold the position for about thirty seconds, then let go of the foot and return to the floor. Repeat this exercise with your right leg.
3. Groin stretch: Sit on the floor and draw your feet into the **groin**, pressing the soles of the feet together so that the knees fall outward. Take hold of your ankles with your hands, and push down on the knees using your elbows. The stretch is concentrated along the inside of the groin. Hold the stretch for about twenty seconds, then gently release the pressure on your knees and bring them up to the center.
4. Side stretch: Stand with your legs in an "A" shape two shoulder-widths apart. Keeping your back straight, slide your left hand down the side of your left leg as far as you can. Once you have reached your maximum position, hold it for five seconds, and then slowly come up again to the middle. Then repeat the exercise on the right side. Repeat the set three times.
5. Waist and back stretch: Again stand with your legs in an "A" shape two shoulder-widths apart. Bend straight forward from the waist and lower your torso as far as it will go, keeping your back straight. Holding the legs and gently pulling on them will help you to go down farther. Hold the stretch for about ten seconds, and then move your body upright again. Place your hands against your lower back and stretch your body backward, looking up at the ceiling as you do. Hold for ten seconds, then release.
6. Shoulder stretch: Hold your left arm straight out in front of you and hook your right forearm around the back of the left elbow. Keeping the

This stretch works the muscles along the inside of the groin.

MEDICAL QUESTIONNAIRE

If you answer yes to any of the following questions, you should have a medical checkup before beginning any program of weight training.

- Have you suffered from any sort of heart condition that stopped you from doing physical exercise?
- Do you suffer from asthma?
- Are you on any medication for an existing illness?
- Have you suffered serious injury or illness affecting your spine, neck, bones, or certain body joints?
- Have you ever experienced any chest pains during physical activity?
- Do you suffer from periods of dizziness or fainting?
- Do you have epilepsy or any other condition that results in seizures or loss of consciousness?
- Do you have any other medical condition that might affect your ability to exercise?

left arm straight, use the right arm to pull it across your body until you feel a strong stretch in the shoulder joint. Hold for ten seconds, then release and switch arms.

7. Neck stretch: Standing up straight, lower your chin so that it rests against your chest. You should feel a stretch up the back of your

neck. Hold for five seconds, then release. Next, bend your head backward and look up toward the ceiling. Do not let your head fall too far backward because this can damage the top vertebrae. Instead, feel you are stretching your face up toward the ceiling. Hold for five seconds and release. Finally, twist your head to look left and then right, each time holding the stretch for five seconds.

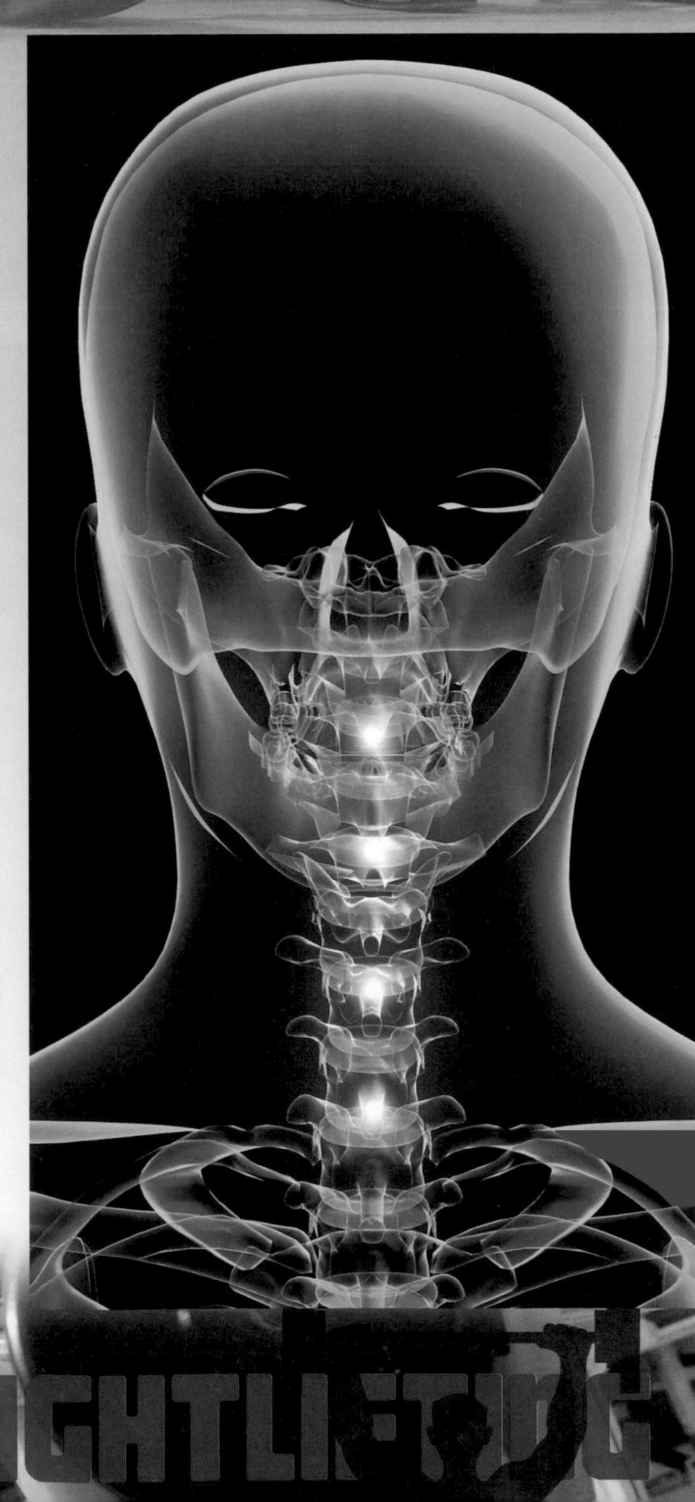

Safe Weight Training

A large percentage of weight-training injuries come from misuse of equipment and the wrong type of training. For anyone younger than eighteen, incorrect

The vertebrae in your neck can be injured during weightlifting. Keep your neck muscles strong and flexible to help avoid injuries.

technique or weight selection can have a very harmful long-term effect on the growing body.

Many experts frown on the idea of weight training for people under the age of eighteen. The main concern is that loading the still-growing body with heavy weight can deform and damage it, leaving the young person with injuries that last a lifetime.

Young people have several important physiological differences from adults, all of which relate to the process of growing. First, during periods of growth, muscles and cartilage are at an increased risk of injury as they stretch to cope with the lengthening of the body. Second, growth makes body joints unstable because muscles around the joints are also adjusting to growth. Finally, the skeleton itself is stretching. In the long bones of the body (such as those that are found in the legs and arms), there are "growth plates," special sections of the bone that enable it to lengthen properly. Loading the growing bones with excessive weight can deform these growth plates and lead to permanent bone damage. Similarly, the growing spine is vulnerable to injury and distortion under heavy weights.

Though these cautions are extremely important, they do not mean that you should never do weight training. Safe weight training for those under eighteen is a matter of learning the correct technique and avoiding dangerous exercises.

THE RIGHT ROUTINE

For young people, the recommended frequency of weight training is two to three sessions per week. Two is the ideal number because it lets you do other forms of exercise during the week. Mixing weight training with sports such as running, swimming, and basketball is also recommended because cross training provides an all-around level of fitness, which helps guard against injury. Doing only weight training may be too hard on your bones, joints, and muscles.

Following safety rules is very important during weight training. If you are under eighteen, these rules become even more important so that you avoid permanently damaging your body.

Adult bodybuilders will attempt to lift the heaviest weights possible as part of their routines. Do NOT attempt this if you are under eighteen; your body is not yet strong enough to support extremely concentrated weight stacks. Gauge the right level of weight for you by the number of repetitions. If you cannot lift, pull, or push a weight with proper technique for eight consecutive repetitions, it is too heavy for you. Instead of aiming to lift large weights, focus on increasing the number of repetitions you do with a weight you can lift comfortably, two sets per exercise.

Steer clear of dead lifts. Dead lifts involve lifting a heavy barbell weight without using a bench, seat, or other support to stabilize you. Your body will undergo dangerous stress during a dead lift, as different muscles throughout the body attempt to keep their balance under the sudden weight.

All weight training should be done slowly and methodically. When lifting, never snatch or jerk the weight. Instead, move it steadily from the start posi-

Swimming is an excellent form of cross training to ensure that your muscles are in the best shape possible for weightlifting.

Only adult weightlifters should attempt dead lifts, as shown here. Young lifters can subject their bodies to dangerous stress if they attempt lifts like this.

tion to the stop position, and always go through the full range of body motion for the exercise. This is where good technique makes a difference.

GOOD TECHNIQUE

Do not use any machine or attempt any new free-weight lift until an expert has coached you in it. Free weights are especially dangerous. Not only are more muscles required for balance when lifting a free weight, but incorrect technique may result in dropping the weight on yourself as well. This last danger is one reason why you should always have a spotter with you when attempt free-weight lifting.

Some basic principles of technique are applicable to almost all weight-training exercises. These involve how you stand, sit, bend, and breathe. Posture is extremely important in weight training. For example, if you sit in a slouching position while performing an overhead press exercise, the spine is placed under unnatural pressure, like a stick being bent until it snaps. If you sit straight, however, the vertebrae of the spine distribute the pressure evenly and naturally. To achieve the proper sitting position, push your buttocks to the very back of the seat and keep your back straight. Lift your chin up, and pull your shoulders back to avoid slouching. Your feet must be flat on the floor and slightly back toward your thighs.

Note that the correct upper-body sitting position is also the correct upper-body standing and bending position. Learning how to sit and stand properly is valuable because it affects your ability to handle weights safely. For example, a popular weight training exercise is the barbell squat. Here, a barbell is held behind the neck and across the shoulders, using an overhand grip. With the weight in this position, the quadriceps, hamstrings, and **gluteals** are exercised by slowly bending the knees until the thighs are parallel to the floor, and then slowly returning to the start position. During this exercise, the back needs to be kept as upright as possible, with the head up and face looking forward; otherwise, the spine will take the pressure of the exercise rather than the leg muscles.

Bending to pick up or handle any weight must be done from the legs and not the back. Try this exercise: place any object (it need not be heavy) on the floor. Stand with your feet close to it and your back straight. Look directly forward. Now bend from your knees and lower yourself down beside the object. At the same time, keep your back as straight as possible. Once you have taken hold of the object, lift your face and look straight forward—this

helps to keep your back upright. Complete the lift by using your legs to push the weight from the floor. If the weight is heavy, keep it close to your stomach, the body's natural center of gravity.

If you are going to take weight training seriously, protecting your back will save you from many problems. Get into the habit of sitting, standing, and bending properly at all times, and those will habits will transfer into the gym.

GOOD BREATHING

Correct breathing is as much a part of good technique as correct posture. Strong breathing maintains the supply of oxygen to the muscles while they are working. The problem with the way many

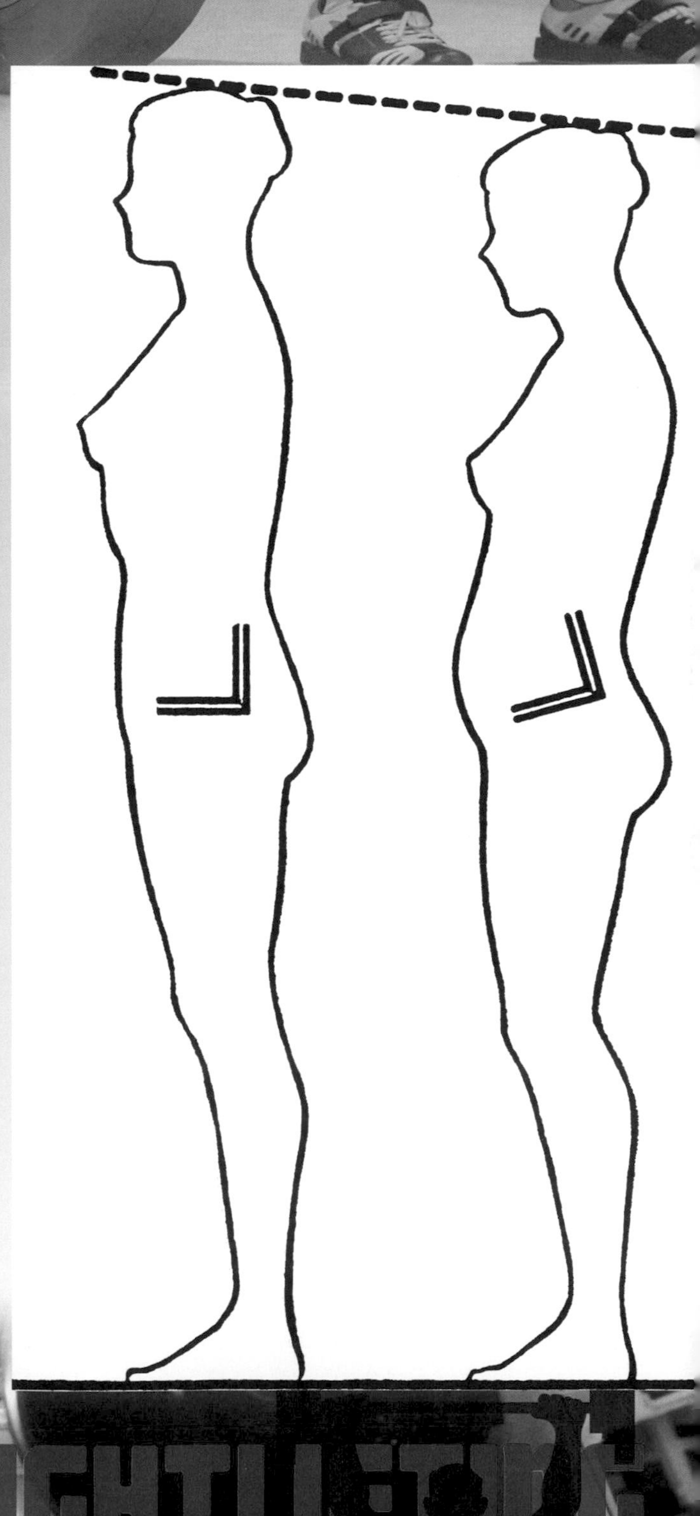

Good posture is important for all weightlifters, both male and female. Practice keeping your stomach in and your pelvis at right angles to the floor.

GYM ETIQUETTE AND PERSONAL SAFETY

- Do not wear jewelry when weight training, particularly necklaces, rings, and earrings. As well as being a hazard to you, some jewelry—especially rings—can stretch or damage the handles of equipment.
- Do not wear excessively baggy T-shirts, which can get caught in machinery. If you are using the rowing machine, tuck your T-shirt into the waistband of your shorts or gym pants to prevent them from getting caught in the runners.
- If using free weights, place them back on the free-weights rack in the same order in which they were arranged. If you have added weights to a bar, it is polite to remove them after use.
- Never leave any litter in the gym, and make sure all bags and personal belongings are safely out of the way.
- When using weight machines, wear good-quality training shoes with rubber nonskid soles to prevent slipping.

of us breathe is that we do not use our lungs to full capacity. This results in a poor input of oxygen to the body. Worse still, while exerting ourselves we have the tendency to hold our breath. This is dangerous during weight training because the combination of held breath and muscular exertion cuts off oxygen in the brain, possibly resulting in a stroke.

It is important to learn proper full-lung breathing. Draw in a deep breathe through your nose. Imagine that you are pulling the breath into your stomach; you will notice that your abdomen inflates first, and then the chest. This sequence indicates that the whole of the lung from bottom to top is filled with air. Exhale from your mouth; the chest will collapse first, followed by the stomach.

Use deep breathing throughout your weight training. However, make sure you follow a specific rhythm. When you lift, pull, or push the weight (known as the "power phase"), breathe out. When you relax the weight back to its starting position, breathe in. This sequence keeps you from holding your breath. The power phase of an exercise should take three full seconds to complete, as should the return phase. Count this rhythm mentally by saying, "one elephant, two elephants, three elephants." Using the word "elephant" ensures that you count in complete seconds. Counting in this way prevents you from using those rapid, jerky movements that are so apt to result in an injury.

4
Common Injuries, Treatment, & Recovery

Understanding the Words

antagonistic muscles: *Pairs of muscle groups that work together by performing opposite actions, such as flexing and extending.*

mobility: *The ability to move easily.*

chronic: *Something that continues for a long time.*

Weight training can have many positive health effects. It aids back problems, weak bones, asthma, and injured knees, as well as other complaints. Yet weight training also has a risk of muscle joint damage if practiced improperly.

Avoid weights that are too heavy, obey the rules of good technique, and develop **antagonistic muscles**, and you will go a long way toward preventing injury. Even so, regular weight training can impose wear and tear on all the joints and muscles. Treating such injuries is a matter of letting the injuries heal naturally, and then strengthening the injured part to withstand further exercise.

Sprains and Strains

Sprains and strains are the most common injuries that happen during weight training. These are usually caused by lifting excessive weight or by poor technique, particularly if you lose your balance during free-weights exercise. The following are the telltale symptoms:

- significant pain in a joint or muscle
- restricted **mobility** in a joint or limb
- swelling or redness around the injury
- a feeling of weakness in a limb at certain ranges of its movement
- trouble getting the injured area comfortable at night
- lack of strength in an injured limb

DID YOU KNOW?

A strain involves a partial or full tear of the muscle or tendon and feels similar to a sprain but with more bruising.

Fortunately, the vast majority of sprains and strains can be treated without the help of a doctor. The initial stages of self-treatment can be remembered by thinking of the word "P.R.I.C.E.," which stands for Protection, Rest, Ice, Compression, and Elevation:

PROTECTION

If you are injured, stop training immediately, and protect the injured area from further damage by restricting all unnecessary activity. If, for example, you have sprained your shoulder, avoid exercises such as bench presses, dumbbell flyes, or pec workouts.

Pain in a joint or in the muscles surrounding a joint is an indication of injury.

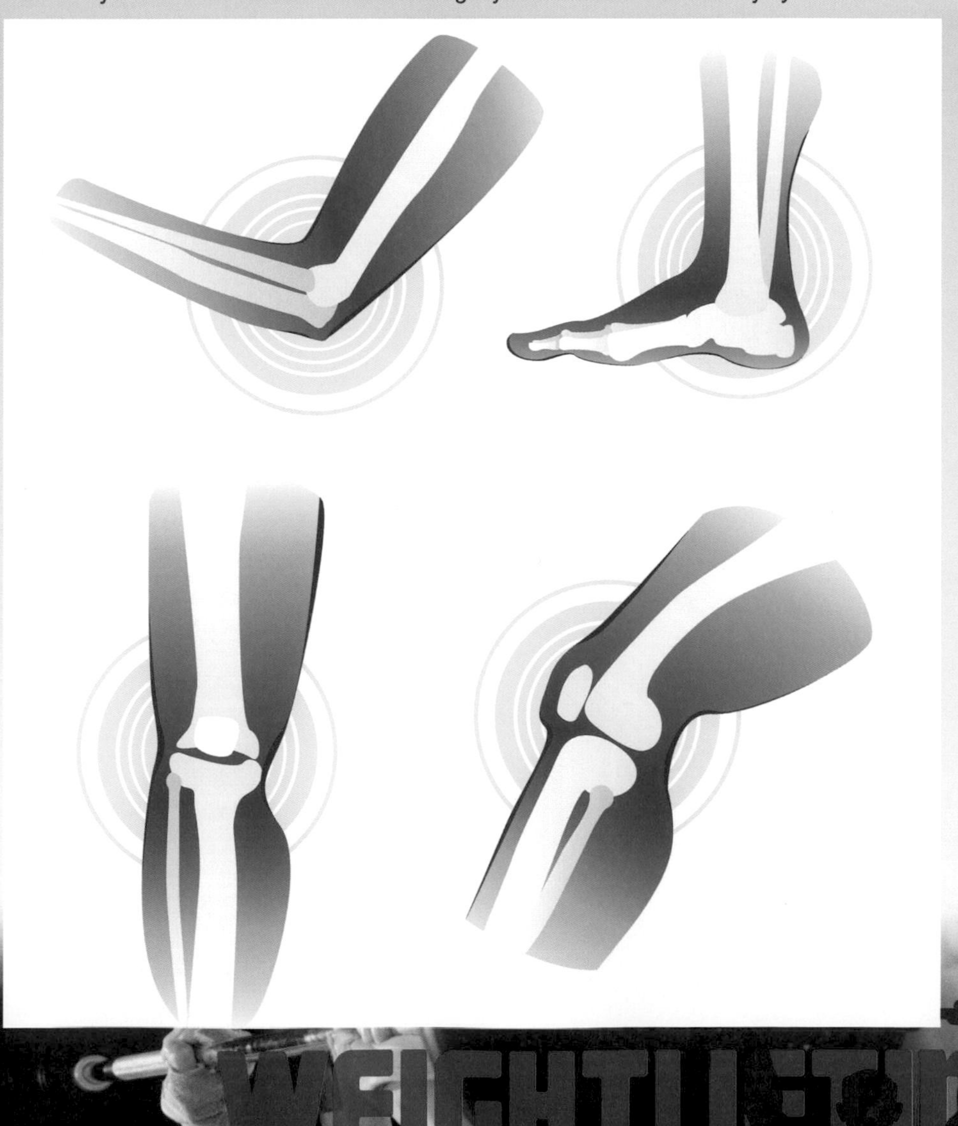

REST

Give the injured area complete rest for at least a week. This does not mean that you have to stop training. An injured knee need not prevent you from doing upper-body training on seated weight machines. Make sure that whatever training you continue to do, no further strain is placed on the injured part. Restrict other activities and sports that affect the injury.

ICE

Reduce any swelling around the injury by applying ice packs about two or three times a day, for no longer than twenty minutes each time. If there is no swelling, you might find it more beneficial to apply heat treatments. Heat-generating ointments are available from sports shops and drug stores, and they are particularly useful for reducing pain in muscle strains. Do not use heat treatments on swelling areas.

Ice helps to reduce the swelling of a strain or sprain.

OVERUSE INJURIES

Repeating the same action many times may cause an overuse or chronic injury. This is not as serious as an acute injury, but any chronic problem may become worse if not acknowledged early on, so weight lifters should seek medical advice and treatment. Overuse injuries have both mental and physical symptoms:

- unusual tiredness or fatigue
- a lack of appetite
- an inability to sleep at night
- muscle soreness and cramps
- stiff, painful or unstable joints
- problems getting part of the body comfortable in bed at night
- painful tendons
- pain that shows no improvement after three days.

COMPRESSION

Wrap the injury firmly in an elastic bandage or, ideally, a professional compression bandage. Applying strong support to a strain or sprain reduces swelling and also protects the joint or muscle from further damage.

ELEVATION

Elevate an injured limb on a surface such as a chair or table that is well padded with cushions. If your leg is injured, try to raise it higher than the hips;

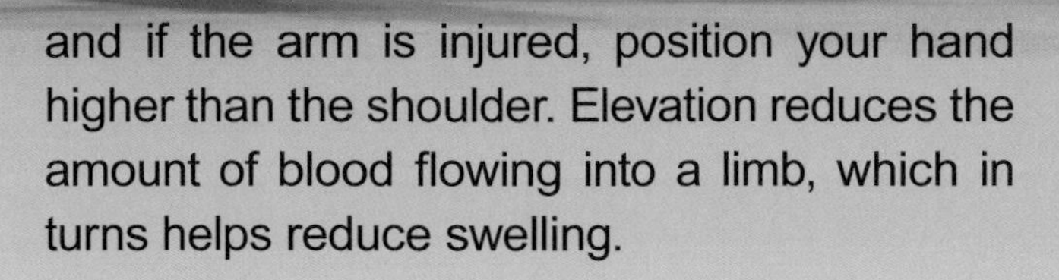

and if the arm is injured, position your hand higher than the shoulder. Elevation reduces the amount of blood flowing into a limb, which in turns helps reduce swelling.

SEVERE DAMAGE

If a sprain or strain is fairly slight, P.R.I.C.E. alone will usually cure it within a week. For more severe damage, however, there are two other stages of rehabilitation. Once the pain has subsided and you feel mobility returning to the joint or limb, it is time to introduce what are known as range of motion (R.O.M.) exercises. These are light stretching and flexibility exercises meant to give the joint or limb its full range of movement. The stretches used should be gentle, but should explore every direction of movement you had before the action.

Once you have full, pain-free R.O.M., you need to strengthen the injured joint or muscle. Fortunately, doing weight training means that you will already know exercises to strengthen the injured part of the body. Here again, the key point is that you do all the exercises gently. Use very light weights of 1 to 3 pounds (.45 to 1.36

Something as simple as a glass of water can help your muscles repair themselves after a workout. Keep yourself hydrated, and your muscles will more quickly lose their soreness after a workout.

ACHES AND PAINS

Do not treat every ache and pain that follows weight training as an injury. Any sport may result in a phenomenon known as delayed-onset muscle soreness (DOMS.) DOMS happens one or two days after strenuous exercise and is caused by the healing of those tiny tears in the muscle tissue that were incurred during training. Usually the ache will disappear within forty-eight hours. However, if it persists for more than three days, you should see a doctor.

Remember to drink plenty of water before, during, and after your weight training session. This helps muscles lose their soreness after exercise because they will rehydrate quicker.

kg), with no strenuous or rapid movements. Build the weight up gradually over a period of several days until you are back to normal levels. Stop training or reduce the weights used if the pain returns.

Rotator Cuff Injury

Weight training imposes particularly heavy strains upon the shoulders. In many upper-body weight-training exercises, the shoulders are required to make powerful lifts, which puts considerable stress on the shoulder joint and surrounding muscles. A common injury is a damaged rotator cuff. The rotator cuff is a group of muscles and ligaments holding the shoulder's ball-and-socket joint together and controlling the arm's rotational movement. About 75 percent of shoulder injuries in weight training are caused by damage to the rotator cuff.

The first stage in treatment is to give the joint complete rest. Stop doing any upper-body weight-training exercises that use the injured shoulder, even with light weights. Keep arm activity to a minimum until the pain in the shoulder has subsided. This may take about a week.

R.O.M. EXERCISES

Now it is time for R.O.M. exercises. One particularly good R.O.M. exercise for the shoulder is called "the pendulum":

1. Stand up and bend over from the waist, supporting yourself by putting a hand against the wall or on a table or other stable object (use the arm on the uninjured side).

Doing this exercise can help you recover your range of motion after a shoulder injury.

2. Hang the arm on the injured side straight downward like a pendulum. Relax the shoulder muscles.
3. Make gentle swinging motions with the arm, forward and back, side to side, and in circles. Change the direction of the swing after about twenty times of using each pattern, and also the direction of the circles.

The pendulum will help free up a stiff shoulder and will relax damaged muscles. If the pendulum causes no pain, do as many different shoulder stretches as you can design. The only rule is that you do not put any strain or force on the shoulder.

For strength training, a single dumbbell about 2 lbs 3 oz (1 kg) in weight is an ideal piece of equipment. For the shoulder try the following exercises:

- Hold the dumbbell to the side of the body, then raise your arm straight out to the side until it is at shoulder height. The thumb should be pointing downward. Hold for three seconds, and then gently lower. Repeat two more times.
- Hold the dumbbell to the side of the body, and then swing it forward with a straight arm so that the weight is level with your shoulder. Hold for three seconds and gently lower, then repeat.

Most strains and sprains are healed by following the above principles or by adapting them to the particular injury. You should always consult a doctor if your efforts do not work. Signs that you need professional help include **chronic** pain; a limb or joint freezing up or losing mobility, despite flexibility exercises; tingling sensations or numbness in the hands or toes; headaches; and nausea or fatigue following the injury.

PAIN: YOUR MINDSET MATTERS

Athletes experiencing a great deal of pain from an injury can learn to control their pain with coping strategies. These include meditation, visualization, and positive thinking. Scientists did a study in which half of patients with back pain were given coping strategies and the other half were not. Those patients who were taught coping strategies dealt with pain much more easily than those who were given no instruction. Your mindset is more important for your recovery than you may think!

Torso Injuries

If you are practicing lifting heavy weights, the other danger you might face is injury to the abdomen and back. During a heavy lift, the muscles of these two areas are placed under tremendous strain. Sometimes the strain is too much and the muscles rupture. The first sign of ruptured abdominal muscles is usually a sharp and violent pain in the abdomen when making a heavy lift. The stomach becomes painful to the touch, and any activity that uses the abdominal muscles, even walking, is difficult.

Except in the case of major rupture, a good two weeks of rest will usually be enough to heal the injury. Avoid body positions in which the legs are stretched out straight while lying on your back. This position may increase the tension in the already sensitive muscles. The healing process is aided by the use of heat packs applied to the stomach area; anti-inflammatory medicines should help bring down any swelling.

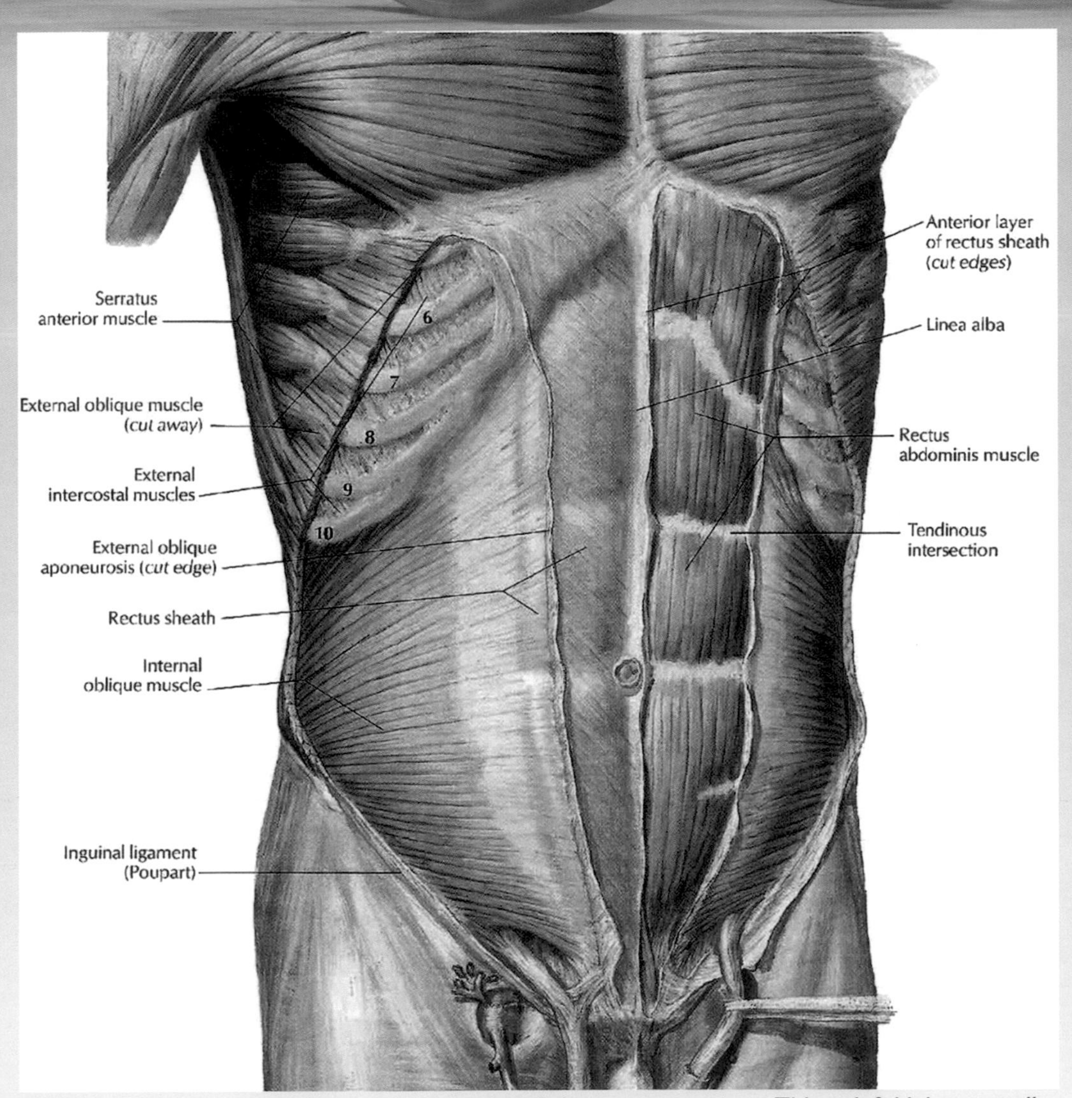

Under very severe stress, the muscles in your abdomen can rupture. This painful injury usually responds to rest.

Exercises for the R.O.M. stage of healing are basic:

1. Stand straight up with your feet shoulder-width apart. Then gently run your left hand down the side of your left thigh, stretching the torso over to the side. Repeat on the right side. Do this set of exercises about three times.
2. Place your hands on either side of your spine in the small of your back. Lean the upper body gently backward while looking upward at the ceiling. As your body arches, the abdominal muscles are stretched.

Practice these exercises for two weeks, then gradually introduce very light abdominal weight training. As with any injury, consult a doctor if the pain does not go away or is particularly acute.

Back injuries are similar in many ways to abdominal injuries. At a moment of strain or twisting, pain will shoot through the back muscles. The pain is made worse through movement or lifting, and the back and neck become stiff and difficult to move. Again, the usual course of treatment is rest, aided by heat treatments and painkilling or inflammatory medication (either over-the-counter or prescribed by a doctor).

As the initial strain becomes bearable, introduce light exercise to increase the back's flexibility and strength. For about a week, do gentle stretches of exactly the same type described for abdominal injuries. Next, do light warm-up routines and undemanding stomach crunches to strengthen the back muscles.

Consult a doctor immediately if you are in any doubt or have other symptoms such as nausea, dizziness, or blood in your urine. In short, treat abdominal or back injuries yourself only if the pain is manageable and you retain some degree of movement.

AGE

Younger athletes are less likely to injure themselves than older ones. Children do not have the strength in their muscles to cause the overuse injuries or accidents that are common to older teens. As teens get older and grow muscle mass, they need increased attention and education about sports injuries.

5 Nutrition and Supplements

Understanding the Words

nutritionist: *A person trained in nutrition and able to help people learn about the best foods to eat.*

metabolism: *The chemical processes necessary for life that occur within the body, including breaking down substances to be used by the cells and creating new substances. The word metabolism is also used informally to refer to how quickly the body performs these processes.*

synthesis: *Combining separate materials or parts into a different, more complex substance.*

When we look at a bodybuilder with huge muscles that are toned perfectly, we know that person not only followed a rigorous workout regimen but also regulated his diet for years. Achieving remarkable amounts of muscle mass requires intense amounts of discipline. The benefits of maintaining healthy nutrition are greater than making a bodybuilder strong; they also help lessen the chances of injury.

When the body trains, it breaks down and rebuilds muscle. Eating right is central to gaining muscle mass and staying healthy. Weightlifters must eat a proper blend of nutrients to make sure their bodies perform as well as possible. Eating right doesn't just mean eating healthy foods, but also choosing when to eat, how much to eat, and whether to take dietary supplements. Eating healthy also does not mean eating less; in fact, the opposite can be true.

Of course, when you switch to a radically different diet or add nutritional supplements, you should consult a **nutritionist**, doctor, or other expert. Making up your own nutrition program can be dangerous.

It takes plenty of nutrition to build and maintain muscles like these.

What to Eat

While a balanced diet is important for everyone, it is even more important for athletes. An athlete eats considerably more than non-active people. The average American eats 2000 calories a day, but an athlete who wants to gain large amounts of muscle mass could eat a very large amount—between 3,000 and 4,000 calories—and continue to gain more muscle than fat.

There are three main food groups to consider when choosing a diet: carbohydrates, protein, and fats.

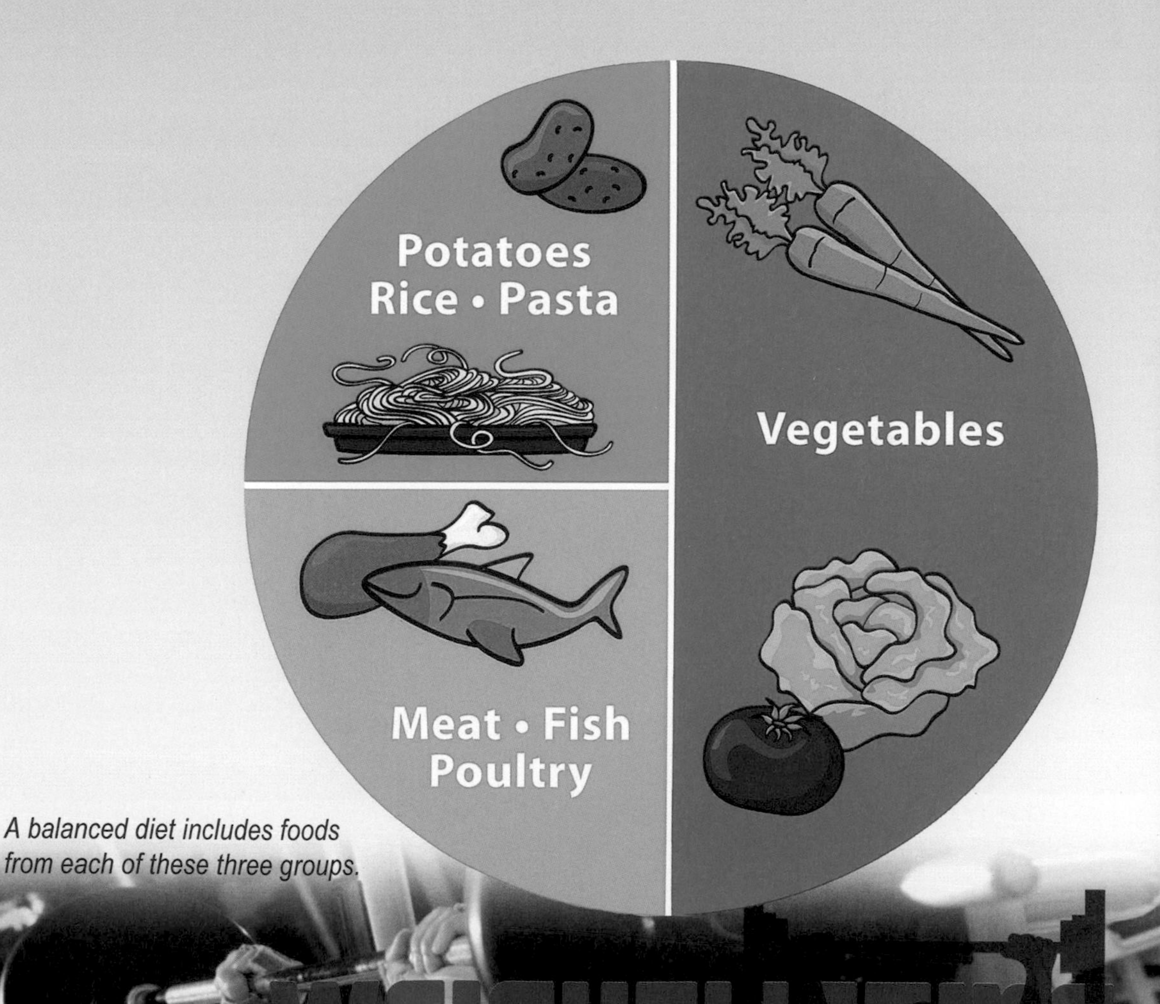

A balanced diet includes foods from each of these three groups.

SIMPLE WAYS TO EAT COMPLEX CARBS

Keep these pointers in mind to make sure you're getting the right carbohydrates:

- Make half of your grains whole. Check the nutrition facts on bread, pasta, and cereal. Make sure the word "whole" is in the first ingredient and avoid the word "enriched" on the back. Because complex carbohydrates are popular, labels misleadingly call foods whole grain when they are not.
- Eat five servings of fruit per day, and another five of vegetables.

CARBOHYDRATES

Carbohydrates provide energy to the body. Between 50 and 65 percent of an athlete's diet should be carbohydrates. Think of carbohydrates (also known simply as "carbs") as the fuel you need to keep your body running through workouts and tournaments.

There are two types of carbohydrates: simple and complex. Simple carbohydrates break down faster and provide a burst of energy but bring your body down fast. Usually they are full of empty calories: food that doesn't nourish the body but has a high amount of calories. Most teenagers know and love simple carbohydrate foods—candy, soda, and other sweets—but an athlete should avoid these foods. Some fruits, such as bananas, are simple carbohydrates and are filled with other vitamins and minerals as well as fiber, but bananas are an exception. While athletes should avoid empty-calorie foods at all times, they should especially steer clear of these foods before workouts to avoid a "crash"—a sudden lack of energy while they work out.

Complex carbohydrates break down more slowly in the body and provide it with more nutrients. Vegetables, fruits, brown rice, whole-grain bread, beans, nuts, and cereal all contain complex carbohydrates. These complex carbohydrates give the body a more sustainable boost of energy. Health professionals agree that switching from simple to complex carbohydrates is one of the smartest dietary choices a person can make. This can be as simple as buying whole-grain pasta instead of lighter kinds at the supermarket. Most complex carbohydrate foods are good sources of fiber, which makes the body feel more full. This, in turn, helps weight loss.

A candy bar can provide you with quick energy, but the energy only lasts for a brief spurt and is often followed by a "crash."

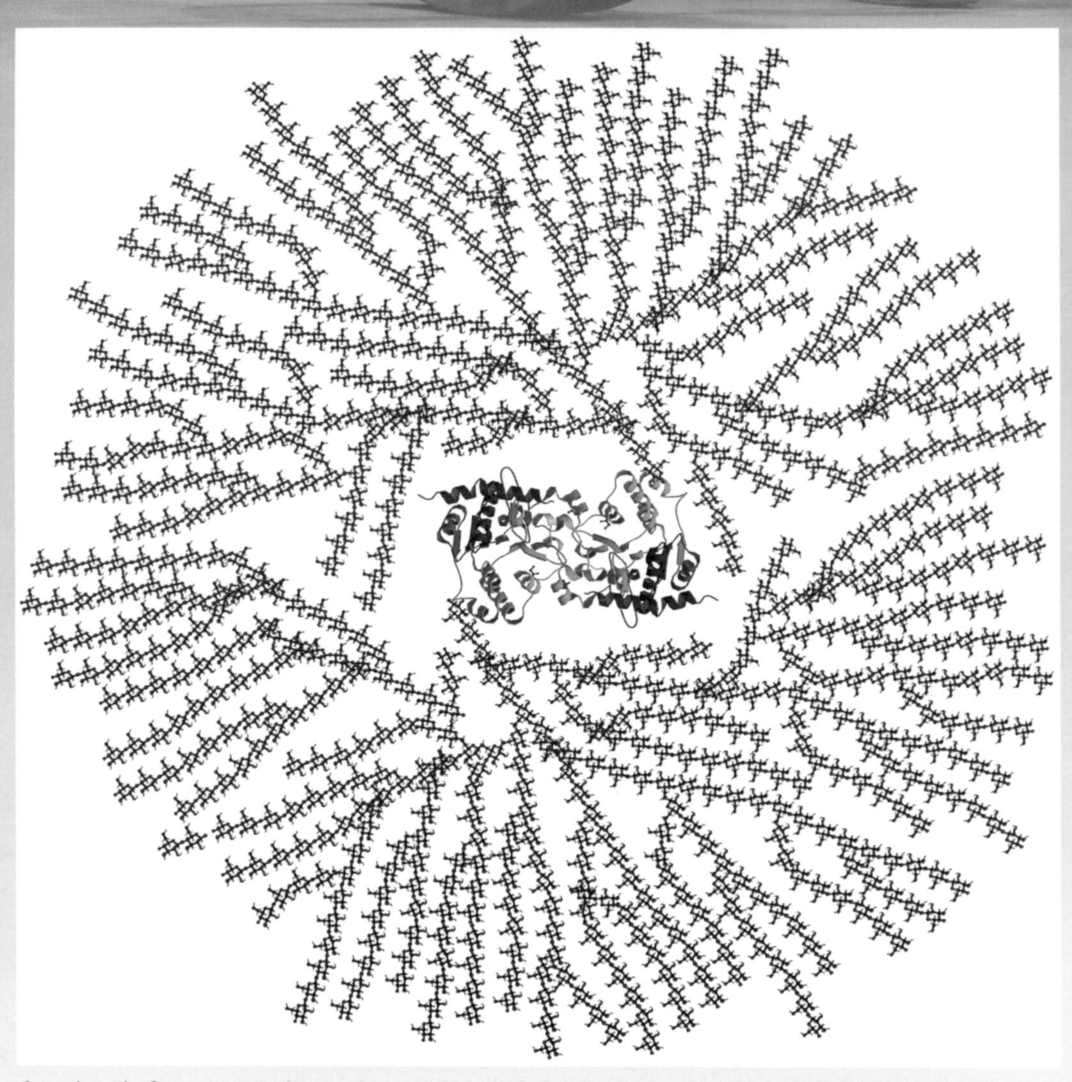

A molecule from a complex carbohydrate, such as what would be found in whole grains or vegetables. Because these molecules do not break down as quickly as simple carbohydrates, the energy they provide lasts longer.

PROTEIN

Proteins are important chemicals found in all living things. The chemicals are used to perform functions inside our body's cells. Each protein is a long, folded, chain like molecule made up of "links" called amino acids. Our bodies break down proteins found in foods and build new proteins that give the body the building blocks needed to become strong. The best sources of proteins are meats and dairy products (like milk or cheese), as well as eggs and certain vegetables (such as soy beans and rice). A good rule of thumb for how much protein to eat is that the number of grams should be equal to about one-third of your body weight in pounds. For example, a 200-pound person should eat about 70 grams of protein every day. Or a 120-pound person should have 40 grams of proteins.

Eggs are a good source of protein, which your body needs in order to repair muscle tears after a workout.

FATS

Although people often think they should avoid fat altogether, fats actually help build up the body and can be used as sources of energy. Healthy skin, teeth, and hair require a steady diet of fats. Also nerve function requires a somewhat fatty diet. Fatty foods should make up no more than 25 percent of your caloric intake, however.

The kinds of fat one consumes make a difference; not all fats are alike. Fats can be classified as polyunsaturated, monounsaturated fats, and saturated fats. Unsaturated fat is good for the body, while saturated fats are best avoided. Foods such as nuts, avocados, canola, and olive oil are all high in Monounsaturated fats (MUFA). These foods help contribute to weight loss. Polyunsaturated fats such as salmon, fish oil, corn, and soy lower cholesterol. Omega 3 fatty acids are polyunsaturated and are found in fish oil. Fish oil can offer benefits such as healthier heart performance and cancer prevention. Omega 3 can even improve one's mental health.

On the other hand, excessive fat intake can have negative effects, especially if you're eating too much saturated fat. Meat, dairy, eggs, and seafood all contain saturated

Fast foods are often high in unhealthy fats.

WATER

Before and after you work out, weigh yourself. If your body lost weight, drink a cup of water for every pound that you lose.

fats. Other oils such as coconut oil and palm oil also have "bad fat." Trans fats were created by scientists to preserve foods longer on the shelf. Many packaged foods like chips and microwavable popcorn contain trans fats. Fast-food restaurants commonly put trans fats in their foods. The health effects of eating trans fat are numerous and range from obesity and heart disease to infertility in women and even Alzheimer's. All these saturated fats contribute to a sluggish feeling after they are eaten. Any kind of fat takes

Avocados are a good source of healthy MUFA fats.

from three to five hours to fully digest—so stock up on carbohydrates for energy instead of any fatty foods.

WATER

Water has been called the most important of all nutrients. The body is made up of 60 percent water, and all parts of the body depend on water to function. Water is so important that the body can only go for 48 hours without it, whereas it can survive for weeks without food.

> **A COMMON MISTAKE**
>
> *One in three Americans think they are hungry when they are actually thirsty. Before you get that midnight snack, make sure to drink a glass or two of water and then see if you still feel hungry.*

By hydrating (filling with water) ourselves, we rejuvenate all parts of our body, including the brain. Water transports nutrients around the body and helps regulate temperature and **metabolism**. You should drink water before, during, and after exercise. Weight lifters should drink eight glasses of water a day.

By hydrating, a bodybuilder is healthier and also is prepping his body for optimum performance to gain muscle mass. Drinking water actually makes you stronger, and even a small amount of dehydration can decrease strength by 15 percent. To maximize intensity of workouts, an athlete needs to be hydrated. The whole process of muscle gain is aided by water, including breaking down muscle fiber. Water also helps protect joints, assisting synovial fluid in "lubricating" joints in the body.

Dietary Supplements

Weightlifters sometimes try to improve their performance by taking dietary supplements. These are pills or drinks that contain nutrients or chemicals to improve physical health or performance in a competition. Dietary supplements do not include illegal performance-enhancing drugs.

Water is vital for the developmental and maintenance of muscles.

When properly used, supplements can improve overall health and performance. You should always consult a doctor or other expert before taking them. Examples of common supplements include vitamin tablets, creatine, and protein shakes or powder.

VITAMIN TABLETS

Vitamins come in many forms. Some provide only one vitamin or mineral that makes up for a neglected nutrient. There are also multivitamins that offer a combination of vitamins and minerals that are needed daily. A good multivitamin should have close to 100 percent of daily-required minerals and vitamins and should be taken at recommended dosages with water near mealtime.

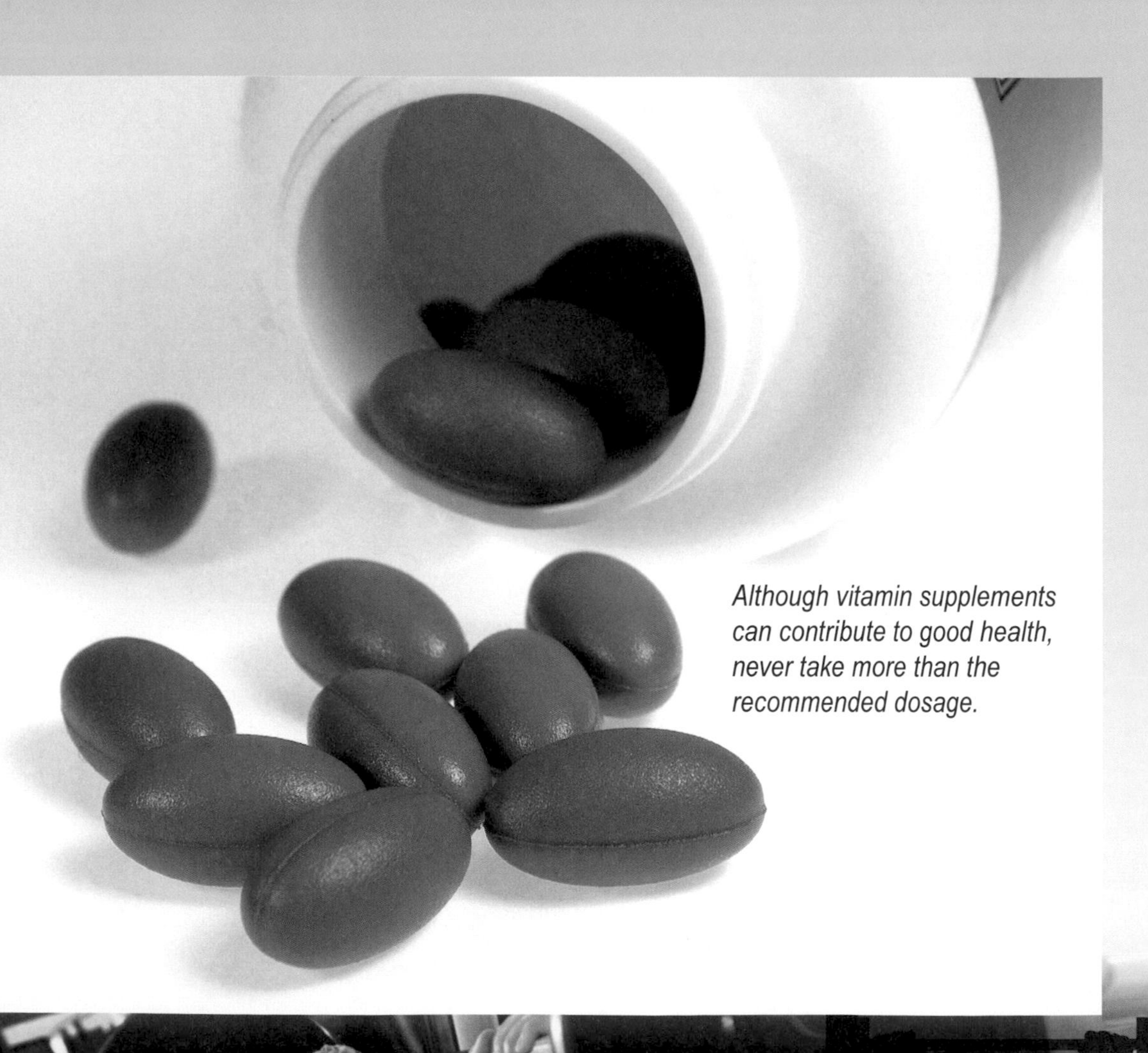

Although vitamin supplements can contribute to good health, never take more than the recommended dosage.

AVOID SCAMS

Make sure when you buy a dietary supplement that it comes from a reputable source. Ask your physician or pharmacist if a certain product can be trusted. In a study in 2004, scientists found that many products that claim to have creatine actually contain none. Even more alarming was that in a separate study in 2001, analysts found out that many chemicals were in muscle-gain products besides the ones that were advertised. Some even included steroids that are harmful to the body and banned from competitive sports.

The eight glasses of water an athlete drinks every day will help her get the most out of vitamins.

But only take the required amount of any vitamin. Any excess vitamin intake will leave the body—or even worse, be stored in the kidneys. What's more, you can overdose on vitamins. Some vitamin supplements are infused with more than is required daily. For instance, B6 vitamins are sold in one-gram quantities, but the body only needs up to two milligrams per day. You should only take a tablet of this amount every two days, since an overdose of vitamin B6 can cause sensory and motor control loss. Other vitamins have equally harmful effects if taken in excess. Vitamin E overdoses cause blood clots, tumors, fatigue, and reproductive problems. While extra Vitamin C flushes out of the body, Vitamin A stores in the kidneys and causes fatigue and dry and itchy skin. When it comes to dietary supplements, there is such thing as too much of a good thing!

CREATINE

Creatine is an attractive dietary supplement for weightlifters because it gives more energy and power during a workout. Creatine is a protein that is naturally found in your body's muscle cells. When taken in larger doses than is found in the body, creatine has the effect of increasing the rate of protein **synthesis** within your body cells. This means that you will have more energy for lifting weights. Creatine does not have the same effect for everyone; between 20 to 30 percent of the general population will not respond to creatine supplements.

Putting any chemical into your body can have negative side effects. You should talk to your doctor before beginning to take creatine. Creatine is only suited for adult athletes; young people seventeen or under should not take it.

PROTEIN SUPPLEMENTS

Getting a sufficient amount of protein from the food you eat can be difficult. To refuel your body, eating protein immediately after a workout is recommended. Most people do not want to cook a meal right after they have pumped iron at the gym, however, so protein shakes are a convenient alternative. Many shakes contain blends of proteins, carbohydrates, fats, and vitamins.

Remember that protein shakes are useful as dietary supplements, not dietary replacements. You can get plenty of nutrients from a balanced diet that can't be replaced by artificial protein shakes.

GINSENG

Ginseng is a natural herb found in Asia that is said to increase alertness and energy. Many do not recommend ginseng for bodybuilding because higher dosages may increase body temperature, unnecessarily increase the heart rate, and possibly cause insomnia.

There is a lack of scientific evidence for ginseng's use in athletics. Most of the studies that showed positive outcomes did not use credible methods. In studies where one group was given real ginseng and others were given pills that did nothing (called placebos), there was almost no difference between those who took the placebo and the real ginseng.

6
The Dangers of Performance-Enhancing Drugs

Understanding the Words

euphoria: *An exaggerated feeling of happiness, confidence, and well-being.*

hormones: *Chemicals secreted by the body that travel through the blood stream and bring about certain actions or reactions.*

paranoia: *The unfounded belief that others are out to get you or that people are working against you.*

delusions: *False beliefs a person is completely convinced of, despite a lack of evidence supporting those beliefs.*

In general, a drug is anything that you place into your body that changes your body's chemistry in some way. Drugs can be useful or beneficial, such as the tablets you might take when you have a headache or antibiotics developed to fight diseases. However, many drugs can have serious negative effects on your health.

Steroids

The goal of weightlifting is to build up your body to perform at a maximum level of strength. Because of this, steroid use is prevalent among weightlifters, especially those who are also interested in bodybuilding.

Anabolic steroids are drugs that chemically resemble androgenic hormones such as testosterone. Steroids work by stimulating receptors found in muscle cells that cause greater muscle growth during a workout.

The idea of being able to multiply the effects of a workout by taking a drug is attractive and difficult to resist. The following are three important reasons, however, not to take steroids:

- Steroids ruin reproductive functions. Testosterone is essential for producing sperm and maintaining a healthy sexy drive. The natural production of testosterone is impaired by the abuse of steroids. When a bodybuilder abuses steroids, they disrupt the way his reproductive system functions. Shrunken testicles, decreased sperm count, impotence, decreased sex drive, and infertility can occur because of steroid abuse. Some studies even suggest that some of these effects do not go away even after a man has stopped taking steroids. For women,

STEROID USE CAN BE FATAL

Steroid-related deaths can occur. Suicide, liver disease, heart attack, and cancer are all more likely to happen to someone who takes steroids.

Steroids trigger the body's normal response to male hormones, increasing muscle production. However, the ultimate effects of steroids can be dangerous, even life-threatening.

DIFFERENCE BETWEEN LEGAL AND NON-LEGAL STEROID USE

Steroids have legal and legitimate uses. After surgeries in which muscle tissue is lost, doctors may prescribe steroids to encourage muscle regrowth. After surgery for testicular cancer, men may be prescribed steroids to make up for lost testosterone. Steroids also help decrease inflammation

Legal steroid use differs from illegal abuse in amount as well as purpose. Doctors prescribe much smaller doses of steroids than what athletes often use. The typical steroid abuser takes eight to ten times the maximum recommended dose of steroids.

menstrual irregularities, baldness, fetal damage, excessive hair growth, sterility, and reduction of the breasts can occur as a result of steroid use.

- Steroids cloud the mind. While scientific studies have not verified that "'roid rage" (an uncontrollable violent urge) as it is portrayed in the media is an effect of taking steroids, they *have* found a higher amount of irritability, aggressiveness, **euphoria**, hyperactivity, and recklessness in steroid abusers. They have also found that steroid abusers often suffer from depression.

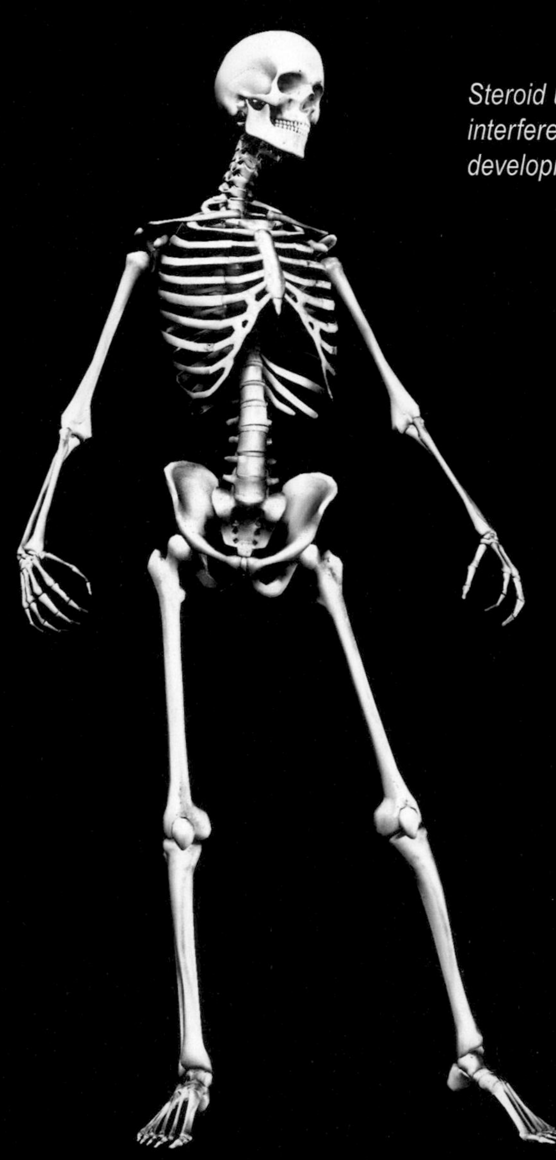

Steroid use during adolescence can interfere with the normal growth and development of your skeleton.

ALCOHOL ABUSE

Many people drink alcohol in our society, but the detrimental effects of alcohol abuse are much worse for athletes than for people who are inactive. When an athlete performs within 48 hours of drinking just two or three standard alcoholic drinks, his body will have impaired reaction time, impaired balance, decreased aerobic capacity, and increased fatigue. The cellular repair of his body is also compromised—and cell repair of muscle tissue is vital for weightlifters and bodybuilders. Alcohol also depletes the body of vitamins and minerals as well as water, things that are needed for the process of muscle growth and maintenance. Finally, alcohol is both fattening and increases fat storage. Drinking disrupts the way in which the body burns fat. The effects of alcohol completely negate a healthy lifestyle. Bottom line: if you are serious about weightlifting, abusing alcohol is not worth it!

- Steroid abuse is illegal. Since 1991, possession of illegally obtained steroids carries a maximum penalty of one year in prison and a minimum fine of $1,000 for a first drug offense. The maximum penalty for selling steroids is five years in prison and a $250,000 fine for a first offender. Most weightlifting competitions ban steroid use.

NEGATIVE EFFECTS FOR TEENS

While steroids take a terrible toll on the adult body, they cause even more damage to teenagers' bodies. The bones of a steroid abuser do not grow

Steroids can cause you to go bald early. They can also make your negative emotions—such as sadness and anger—become stronger and harder to handle.

CIGARETTE SMOKING

Smoking cigarettes gets in the way of weight training. The heartbeat of a smoker is 30 percent faster on average than a non-smoker; this extra amount of effort that the heart is required to make is a detriment to competing in weightlifting. Even worse, tobacco reduces the amount of oxygen available to muscles during exercise. Instead, smoking encourages the replacement of oxygen with carbon monoxide and causes oxygen depletion and reduction in performance. Phlegm production in smokers is doubled, so mucous forms in the airways and gets in the way of breathing—which is crucial for weightlifting. While exercising increases oxygen intake by 20 percent, people who smoke only get a 10 percent benefit from a workout. Not only will smoking dramatically increase your chance of getting cancer from the harmful substances in cigarettes—but it will lessen your ability to lift weights.

as much as they should, and the changes undergone through puberty can be accelerated. A teen who takes steroids before he is fully grown could risk being shorter than he would have been otherwise.

Severe acne, trembling, and high blood pressure are other side effects of steroid use in teens. Jaundice, which is a yellowish coloring of the skin caused by the liver not working correctly, is also a side effect, as is an increase in high-blood pressure. In some cases, steroids can cause kidney and liver

REAL-LIFE WEIGHTLIFTER

When Naim Suleymanoglu was only sixteen years old, he set the first world record of his career by lifting three times his own body weight in the clean-and-jerk event. He was only the second lifter in the history of weightlifting to achieve this.

Suleymanoglu was often called "The Pocket Hercules" because of his small physique. In the 1988 Seoul Summer Games, Suleymanoglu competed for Bulgaria in the featherweight weightlifting competition and won the first Olympic title of his career. In 1989, he won the World Weightlifting Championships. After the 1989 World Championships, Suleymanoglu announced his retirement from the sport—but he returned to competitive weightlifting in 1991. In the 1992 Barcelona Summer Olympics, he won the second Olympic gold medal of his career. In his next appearance at the 1996 Atlanta Summer Games, Suleymanoglu won his third Olympic title in the featherweight weightlifting event. After the 1996 Games, he again retired from the sport.

tumors in teens. Steroids affect **hormones** adversely as well; for males, steroids can cause baldness and breast development.

A teenage athlete on steroids will also have a harder time coping with the emotional experience of growing up. While steroids make the athlete feel good about the size of his muscles, severe mood swings accompany this short-term confidence boost. Depression, sometimes even life-threatening depression, is often seen after steroids have been stopped. This makes steroids difficult to quit, like any other addictive drug. Other mental problems such as **paranoia**, **delusions**, and jealousy can accompany steroid use.

Diuretics

Any sport that involves a "weigh-in"—where there are classes of competition based on weight—carries the risk of diuretic abuse. Many athletes who abuse diuretics for this reason also follow other self-abusive weight-loss practices. Examples include starvation diets and sweating pounds off in rubber suits or saunas. If diuretics are abused along with these unhealthy practices, the athlete is at risk for severe dehydration, seizures, and even death.

Diuretics are also used to mask the abuse of other substances like steroids. By taking a diuretic, the body flushes out many of the traces of other drugs. Because of this, many officiators at weightlifting competitions test for diuretic use.

Quick Fix, Lasting Pain

Want to have huge muscles? Then choose your diet carefully and follow your coach's instructions. Taking performance-enhancing drugs just isn't worth it!

Sure, there are short-term benefits for taking steroids and other performance-enhancing drugs. Otherwise, no one would take them. However, the risks are so extreme that they undo any potential benefits. Performance-enhancing drugs destroy the body; they don't improve it.

Ultimately, life is more important than winning weight competitions or buffing up for any sport. Drugs can damage your body. They can even take your life. They simply aren't worth it.

Further Reading

Delavier, Frederic. *Strength Training Anatomy, 3rd Edition*. Champaign, Ill.: Human Kinetics Publishers, 2010.

El-Hewie, Mohamed F. *Essentials of Weightlifting and Strength Training.* Lodi, N.J.: Shaymaa Publishing, 2006.

Everett, Greg. *Olympic Weightlifting: A Complete Guide for Athletes and Coaches.* Sunnyvale, Calif.: Catalyst Athletics, 2009.

Kennedy, Robert. *Encyclopedia of Bodybuilding: The Complete A–Z Book on Muscle Building.* Mississauga, Canada: Robert Kennedy Publishing, 2008.

McCauley, Don. *Power Trip: A Guide to Weightlifting for Athletes, Parents, and Coaches*. Indianapolis, Ind.: Dog Ear Press, 2010.

Schuler, Lou, Cassandra Forsythe, and Alwyn Cosgrove. T*he New Rules of Lifting for Women: Lift Like a Man, Look Like a Goddess*. New York: Avery Trade, 2008.

Schuler, Lou and Ian King. *The Book of Muscle: The World's Most Authoritative Guide to Building Your Body*. Emmaus, Penn.: Rodale, 2003.

Zatsiorsky, Vladimir and William Kraemer. *Science and Practice of Strength Training, 2nd Edition*. Champaign, Ill.: Human Kinetics Publishers, 2006.

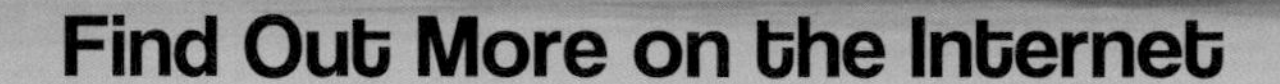

Find Out More on the Internet

Beginner Weight Training
www.mensfitness.com/fitness/beginner_weight_training

Bodybuilding Tips
www.bodybuildingtipsguide.com

International Weightlifting Federation
www.iwf.net

Lift Up: History of Olympic Weightlifting
www.chidlovski.net/liftup

Mike's Gym, USA Weightlifting Regional Training Center
www.mikesgym.org

USA Weightlifting
weightlifting.teamusa.org

Disclaimer

The websites listed on this page were active at the time of publication. The publisher is not responsible for websites that have changed their address or discontinued operation since the date of publication. The publisher will review and update the websites upon each reprint.

Bibliography

"Creatine FAQs Menu." Creatine Information Center, www.creatinemonohydrate.net/creatineinformation.html (11 May 2010).

SirGan. "Side effects of weight lifting." 12 April 2006. SteadyHealth.com, www.steadyhealth.com/articles/Side_effects_of_weight_lifting_a12_f0.html (10 May 2010).

"Steroid statistics." Association Against Steroid Abuse, www.steroidabuse.com/steroid-statistics.html (11 May 2010).

"Why is water so important for a bodybuilder?" BuildMuscleGainWeight.com, build-muscle-gain-weight.com/the-importance-of-water-intake-for-bodybuilders.html (12 May 2010).

Index

Picture Credits

Creative Commons: p. 61, 66
Cyclonebill, Creative Commons: p. 73
Czapnik, Sebastian; Dreamstime: p. 87
Denniskwaria, Creative Commons: p. 44
Grunow, Michael: p. 71
Harvey, Chris; Dreamstime: p. 85
Hashisho, Ramzi: p. 72
Herreid, Mark; Dreamstime: p. 54
Kaulitzki, Sebastian; Dreamstime: p. 41
Kosmal, Marek; Dreamstime: p. 22
Lepinski, John; Dreamstime: p. 37
Local Fitness, Creative Commons: p. 12
Luchschen, Dreamstime: p. 58
Nicolic, Miodrag; Dreamstime: p. 53
Pobiedziński, Andrzej: p. 69
Raul654, Creative Commons: p. 10
Rogeriopfm, Creative Commons: p. 35
Santana, Elvis: p. 29
Slovac Musclemen, Creative Commons: p. 27
Swanson, Gordon; Dreamstime: p. 75
Szorstki: p. 56
U.S. Airforce: p. 17
U.S. Army: p. 20
U.S. Justice Department: p. 83
U.S. Navy: p. 43, 45
Vof, Corepics; Dreamstime: p. 39

To the best knowledge of the publisher, all images not specifically credited are in the public domain. If any image has been inadvertently uncredited, please notify Harding House Publishing Service, 220 Front Street, Vestal, New York 13850, so that credit can be given in future printings.

About the Author and the Consultants

Jonathan S. McIntosh is a writer living in upstate New York. He graduated from Binghamton University with a degree in English literature. He enjoys making music on his laptop, playing poker, and being a literacy volunteer. Currently, he writes on topics ranging from military history to health and fitness.

Susan Saliba, Ph.D., is a senior associate athletic trainer and a clinical instructor at the University of Virginia in Charlottesville, Virginia. A certified athletic trainer and licensed physical therapist, Dr. Saliba provides sports medicine care, including prevention, treatment, and rehabilitation for the varsity athletes at the university. Dr. Saliba is a member of the national Athletic Trainers' Association Educational Executive Committee and its Clinical Education Committee.

Eric Small, M.D., a Harvard-trained sports medicine physician, is a nationally recognized expert in the field of sports injuries, nutritional supplements, and weight management programs. He is author of *Kids & Sports* (2002) and is Assistant Clinical professor of pediatrics, Orthopedics, and Rehabilitation Medicine at Mount Sinai School of Medicine in New York. He is also Director of the Sports Medicine Center for Young Athletes at Blythedale Children's Hospital in Valhalla, New York. Dr. Small has served on the American Academy of Pediatrics Committee on Sports Medicine, where he develops national policy regarding children's medical issues and sports.